FRIENDS
OF ACPL

HOLIDAY COLLECTION

HAWAIIAN
Night Before
CHRISTMAS

(Ka Pō Ma Mua O Kalikimaka)

HAWAIIAN
Night Before
CHRISTMAS
(Ka Pō Ma Mua O Kalikimaka)

Written and Illustrated by Carolyn Macy

PELICAN PUBLISHING COMPANY
GRETNA 2008

To my family and friends

*The word "Pelican" and the depiction of a pelican
are trademarks of Pelican Publishing Company, Inc.
and are registered in the U.S. Patent and Trademark Office.*

Library of Congress Cataloging-in-Publication Data

Macy, Carolyn.
   Hawaiian night before Christmas / written and illustrated by Carolyn Macy.
      p. cm.
   ISBN-13: 978-1-58980-598-9 (hardcover : alk. paper) 1. Christmas—Hawaii—Juvenile poetry. 2. Hawaii—Juvenile poetry. 3. Children's poetry, American. I. Title.
   PS3613.A2834H38 2008
   811'.6—dc22
                                                        2008004560

Printed in Korea
Published by Pelican Publishing Company, Inc.
1000 Burmaster Street, Gretna, Louisiana 70053

HAWAIIAN NIGHT BEFORE CHRISTMAS
As the balmy trade breezes flowed over the land,
Not a gecko was stirring in the flora and sand.
The *lauhala* were placed with the lānai just in view,
Where plumeria were swaying as soft breezes blew.

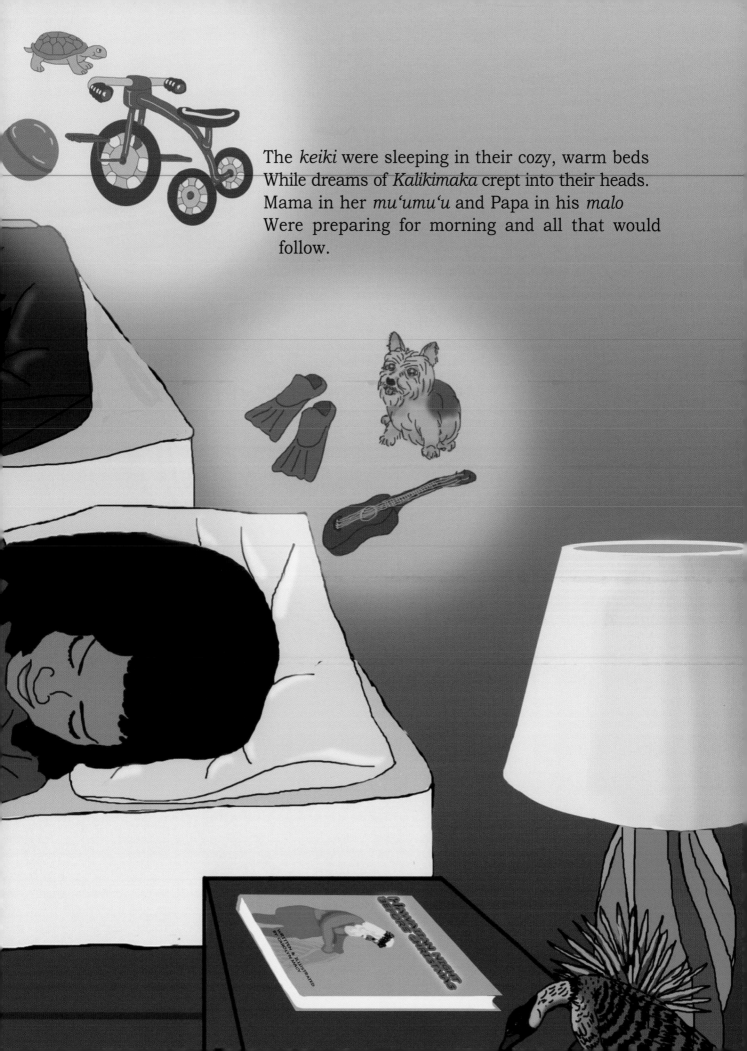

The *keiki* were sleeping in their cozy, warm beds
While dreams of *Kalikimaka* crept into their heads.
Mama in her *muʻumuʻu* and Papa in his *malo*
Were preparing for morning and all that would
    follow.

Their attention was taken by a noise outside
So loud that it muffled the surf on the tide!
Papa ran to the door to search for the sound.
He peered toward the ocean after checking around.

The moon on the spray of the surf in the sea,
And the shine on the sand, as white as could be,

Lighted the way for the cause of the noise:
It looked to be Santa with a net full of toys!

He was perched there aboard an outrigger canoe
That was skimming the waves and pulled by *honu*.
He moved in so quickly past dark Diamond Head,
Urging them onward as quite plainly he said,

"We have gifts to deliver and schedules to keep
And a world of *keiki* now fast asleep.
Surf on, Koa and Keoni, Peka and 'Elele,
On Kumu and Kolohe, Momi and Mele!"

Around each neck was a *kukui nut lei,*
Which helped with the moonbeams in lighting
their way

To the slumbering *keiki* by the shimmering shore:
Straight to the *hale* they flew as in lore.

Across the beach sands with waving palm trees
They hurried and hustled, determined to please.
On this night of all there wasn't much pause
In delivering the toys from dear Santa Claus.

They reached the lānai quickly, stopping just so.
Santa entered the *hale* with presents in tow!

Mele Kalikimaka
Kanakaloka

Aloha

He was dressed in a *malo* and *kāmaʻa nui*
With leis of plumeria, *maile,* and *kukui.*
His whiskers were white as the hair on his head,
And it was surprising how lightly he tread.

His eyes shone like moonlight brightening his face,
And his mustache-framed mouth held a big smile
  in place.

MELE KALIKIMAKA

His *kāma'a nui* he put by the door
Beside all the ones that were placed there before.
Mama greeted Santa with a welcoming lei
To add to the others received on his way.

MELE KALIKIMA

He hummed a soft tune as his night's
  work began.
Santa filled the *lauhala* before stopping to scan
Around the room to the bright coconut tree,
All trimmed and lighted as any could be.

MELE KALIKIMAKA

And like magic the ornaments danced in a ring,
Whispering to Santa the things he should bring.
More presents he placed under its branches aglow
And topped each gift with a beautiful bow.

There on the table, a message he spied.
It said, "Dear Santa, before continuing your
ride . . .

"Please sit for a moment to enjoy this treat
Of macadamia nut cookies so *'ono* and sweet."

He winked once at Papa as he finished them off,
Drank his coconut milk, and gave a small cough.

He slipped on his *kāmaʻa nui* and ran
  out of the door
To the *honu* who were waiting to surf
  on as before.

As he jumped back aboard with a *pū* to his lip,
He signaled the team to continue their trip.
And then he shouted to each *keiki*, be they big or
    quite small . . .

HAWAIIAN-ENGLISH DICTIONARY

aloha (ah-loh-hah)—a greeting: hello, goodbye; love
Diamond Head—volcano crater on Oʻahu
flora—trees and flowers
gecko (geh-koh)—small lizard
hale (hah-lay)—house
honu (hoh-noo)—sea turtles
Kalikimaka (Kah-lee-kee-mah-kah)—Christmas
kāmaʻa nui (kah-mah-ah noo-ee)—large shoes or slippers
Kanakaloka (Kah-nah-kah-loh-kah)—Santa Claus
keiki (kay-kee)—children
kukui (koo-koo-ee)—nuts from the kukui tree in Hawaiʻi
kukui nut lei (koo-koo-ee nuht lay)—necklace made from nuts of the
    kukui tree
lānai (lah-nye)—porch
lauhala (lau-hah-lah)—baskets woven from leaves of the pandanus
    tree, used instead of Christmas stockings
lei (lay)—flowers, seeds, or other things strung into a necklace
maile (my-lay)—a vinelike plant in Hawaiʻi
malo (mah-loh)—cloth wrapped around the hips for men
Mele Kalikimaka (May-lay Kah-lee-kee-mah-kah)—Merry Christmas
muʻumuʻu (moo-oo-moo-oo)—loose-fitting dress or gown
ʻono (oh-noh)—delicious
plumeria (plu-mare-ee-ah)—a flowering tree found in Hawaiʻi
pū (poo)—a large, spiral conch shell used as a trumpet
surf—breaking waves or riding the breaking waves

HONU NAMES DICTIONARY

ʻElele (Ay-lay-lay)—messenger
Keoni (Kay-oh-nee)—God's gift
Koa (Koh-ah)—brave, bold, fearless
Kolohe (Koh-loh-hay)—rascal
Kumu (Koo-moo)—teacher, source
Mele (May-lay)—song, poem, chant, merry
Momi (Moh-mee)—pearl
Peka (Pay-kah)—teller of tales, tattler

HAWAIIAN ISLANDS

Kaua`i
Ni`ihau
O`ahu
Honolulu
Moloka`i
Lana`i   Maui
Molokini
Hawai`i

Santa's Trip ● ● ●